D1271611

Angel
Stories
from the Bible

Under the direction of Romain Lizé, Vice President, MAGNIFICAT

Editor, MAGNIFICAT: Isabelle Galmiche

Editor, Ignatius: Vivian Dudro

Translator: Janet Chevrier

Proofreader: Claire Gilligan

Assistant to the Editor: Pascale van de Walle

Layout Designer: Gauthier Delauné

Production: Thierry Dubus, Sabine Marioni

Original French edition: *Belles Histoires pour s'endormir avec les anges*
© 2013 by Mame, Paris.
© 2017 by MAGNIFICAT, New York • Ignatius Press, San Francisco
All rights reserved.
ISBN Ignatius Press 978-1-62164-207-7. ISBN MAGNIFICAT 978-1-941709-45-0
The trademark MAGNIFICAT depicted in this publication is used under license from
and is the exclusive property of Magnificat Central Service Team, Inc., A Ministry to
Catholic Women, and may not be used without its written consent.

Angel
Stories
from the Bible

Text by Charlotte Grossetête

Illustrations by Madeleine Brunelet,
Sibylle Delacroix, and Éric Puybaret

JESSAMINE COUNTY PUBLIC LIBRARY
600 South Main Street
Nicholasville, KY 40356

MAGNIFICAT · Ignatius

Contents

Jacob's Ladder

Jacob was on his way to Haran. There was a long, lonely road ahead of him, but that didn't scare him. Before he was born, his grandfather Abraham had made a long journey, too, because God had called him to settle in a different country. And now young Jacob, who had never left his parents before, was happy to set off in turn.

His parents! Before sending him to Haran, his elderly father, Isaac, had given him his blessing. And his mother, Rebekah, had hugged him, saying, "Go, my son. You won't find a suitable wife here. The girls of this land don't pray to the Lord, and they do not care about serving him. But you know we must love God with all our might. In Haran, at my brother Laban's house, you will find a bride who loves the Lord as we do. So go!"

With a youthful spring in his step, Jacob took to the road. He walked all day. By sunset he was tired, and he decided to stop for the night. He was in a deserted place dotted with scrawny bushes and stones. The ground was hard and uncomfortable. But no matter! Jacob wasn't hard to please. He found a flat stone to lay his head on and fell right to sleep as though he were lying on the softest of pillows. While in a deep sleep, he had a dream. He saw a ladder rising up from the ground. It was so tall, its top reached up to heaven. Going up and down its rungs were lots of angels. The heavenly beings climbed effortlessly and gracefully, without making a sound. Jacob watched them, marveling at their beauty.

His eyes were soon drawn up to the top, where the Lord was standing in his glory! And the voice of God filled Jacob's soul: "I am the God of your father Abraham and your father Isaac. The land on which you lie, I will give to you and your descendants. Your descendants will be like the dust of the earth and spread far and wide! I am with you and will watch over you wherever you go, and I will bring you back to this land that I have promised you."

Jacob awoke and rubbed his eyes. Still bedazzled, he looked about him for the ladder, the angels, and the splendor of God. But he saw nothing more than the night sky studded with stars. There was total silence. Jacob sat down, frightened. "How awesome is this place!" he said to himself. "This is the house of God and angels! This is the gate of heaven!"

But he calmed himself with the thought of the promise he had just heard. The Lord was his friend. He had nothing to fear. He went back to sleep with this dream engraved on his heart like a precious memory that would stay with him always.

The next day, he woke at dawn. He took the stone he had used as a pillow and set it up as a pillar. Then he poured oil on it to show that it was sacred and made this vow: "If God watches over me on my journey, if I return home safe and sound, this pillar will be a holy place." And he named the place Bethel, which means "house of God."

Then he set off again. He traveled many miles before reaching Haran. When he arrived, he met a shepherdess by a well. It was Rachel, Laban's daughter, giving water to her flock of sheep. She was very beautiful, and Jacob gave thanks to God for having placed her on his path.

Jacob introduced himself to Rachel and asked her where her father was. "Wait for me here; I'll go and get him!" she exclaimed.

She ran to tell Laban, who went to greet his nephew at the well. He embraced him, saying, "You will come and stay with us. What joy to welcome you!"

Jacob followed Laban and Rachel to their home. The more time he spent with Rachel, the more deeply he fell in love with her. Yes, there was no doubt about it: God had kept his promise to make him happy and to help him found a great family!

Raphael and Tobias

Old Tobit had served the Lord his whole life long. He was wise and fair, generous to the poor, and a hard worker, and everyone loved him. Alas, tragedy struck when he was seventy-two years old: He went blind. He could no longer work. He went on praying, but his wife wept at the thought of sinking into poverty.

She wasn't the only one in the land who was weeping. Far away, in the town of Ecbatana, there lived a very unhappy young woman. Sarah had been engaged to be married seven times, but each of her fiancés had died on their wedding day. No one dared to ask for her hand in marriage any more, so Sarah lived with her father, Raguel, and begged God to bring her happiness.

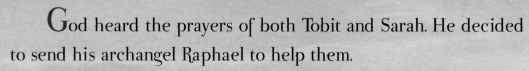

God heard the prayers of both Tobit and Sarah. He decided to send his archangel Raphael to help them.

One day, Tobit said to his son Tobias, "It doesn't matter if we become poor, my son, for the love of God is our real wealth. But I still have ten silver coins. I entrusted them twenty years ago to a man called Gabael who lives in Rages. Find a traveling companion, for you are very young to be traveling on your own, and go get the money. It will make our lives easier."

Tobias left the house and found Raphael standing before him, but he didn't know he was an angel.

"Hello, my friend," said Tobias. "Do you know the way to Rages?"

"I know the way like the back of my hand," replied the angel. "I'll come along with you, if you like."

"I'd like that very much. Thank you! I'll pay you one drachma a day for your assistance."

The angel smiled.

"But tell me, what's your name?" asked Tobias.

"Azarias," replied Raphael.

The two set off with Tobias' dog, which refused to be parted from his master. They walked all day long. When it was evening, they camped along the bank of a river. The next day, they continued on their way. At nightfall, they reached the town of Ecbatana.

"Is it much farther to Rages, brother Azarias?" asked Tobias.

"A two-day walk," Raphael told him. "We'll stop for the night at the home of a man called Raguel."

When they arrived at the house of Raguel, the angel said, "Tobias, I need to tell you something."

"Yes?"

"Raguel has an only daughter called Sarah. She is very big-hearted and has a lively faith in God. You know, her father would be happy if you married her. Why don't you ask her?"

Tobias stared at him and said, "I've heard about her! All of her fiancés have died one after the other! I don't really want to risk—"

"Have no fear, Tobias. If you ask God to protect you, he will."

Tobias and Raphael knocked on Raguel's door, and the man gave them a warm welcome. As soon as Tobias saw Sarah, he fell so in love with her that his heart was won for ever. He asked her to marry him, and the wedding was celebrated there and then. Poor Raguel! He was so worried for his new son-in-law. When the festivities were over, he quietly slipped away to dig a grave, for he was sure that the bridegroom would die that night! Meanwhile, Tobias and Sarah went to their bedroom. They thanked God for their happiness and prayed for his protection. When Raguel sent his servant to see if Tobias were dead, she found them peacefully asleep!

Several days later, Tobias returned to his parents' house. He threw himself in the arms of old Tobit, crying out, "Father, I've brought back your money, but even better than that: I got married to the best of women!"

Tobit was delighted. He embraced his son, saying, "Is she beautiful?"

"You'll see for yourself, Father! For my traveling companion, Azarias, gave me an ointment to heal your eyes. Take courage!"

The young man put the ointment on his father's eyes, and Tobit immediately regained his sight. Tobias turned to Raphael, who was still by his side, and said, "Brother, I owe you more than one drachma per day, because you have made us happy again."

"Do not pay me, but thank God," the angel said. "Know, my friends, that I am Raphael, one of the seven angels who stand for ever before the glory of the Lord."

At these words, the whole family was alarmed and fell to their knees. But Raphael went on, "Do not be afraid. Peace be with you! Bless the Lord, and teach your children to love him. As for me, I am ascending back to him."

With that, Raphael disappeared. Tobias and Sarah would never forget him, and they wrote a book about the wonderful things the Lord had done for them with the help of an angel.

Gabriel's Good News

Gabriel is one of the archangels who live in the glory of God. Like all heavenly beings, he is immortal, and the centuries roll by without aging him.

The Lord made him one of his special messengers. In olden times, God sent him to the prophet Daniel to explain the meaning of his visions.

Six hundred years later, Gabriel returned to earth. This time, God sent him to the priest Zechariah, who had never been able to have children. Gabriel appeared before Zechariah and said to him, "Your wife, Elizabeth, will bear you a son, and you will name him John. He will be filled with the Holy Spirit. He will walk before the Lord with the power of a great prophet, and he will bring many people back to God."

Zechariah replied, "How can I be sure of this? For I am an old man and my wife is aged."

The angel responded a little sharply, "I am Gabriel. I stand in the presence of God, and I have been sent to announce this good news to you. But since you doubt my word, you will remain speechless until the birth of your son."

And everything happened just as Gabriel said.

Six months after his visit to Zechariah, Gabriel was sent to Nazareth, a little village in Galilee, to a young woman named Mary, who was engaged to Joseph. The angel knew that this would be his greatest mission on earth: to announce God's plan to send the Savior, to the woman who would be his mother.

Dawn was breaking on a beautiful day in Nazareth. Mary was already up. She was sewing linens for her future home. The first rays of sunshine lit her face. She didn't at first notice that an angel was standing before her. Gabriel observed her for a moment. There was something gentle and bright about Mary that he had never before seen in a human being. That was why, when she raised her eyes, archangel though he was, he bowed before her.

He said to her, "Hail, Mary, full of grace. The Lord is with you."

Mary was stunned. She clasped her hands, dropping her needle and thread without even noticing.

The angel continued, "Do not be afraid, Mary, for you have found favor in the eyes of the Lord. You will bear a child, and you shall call him Jesus. He will be great, the Son of the Most High. He will be king for ever."

Mary asked, "How will that happen, since I am not yet married?"

The angel recalled Zechariah. Six months ago, the old priest had asked him for proof that what he said was true. But Mary did not doubt. She was surprised, but she already trusted him. The angel Gabriel replied, "The power of the Lord will come upon you, and the Holy Spirit will overshadow you. Your child will be holy, for he will be the Son of God."

And he added, "Your cousin Elizabeth, whom everyone thought barren, in her old age is also expecting a son. For nothing is impossible for God!"

Mary replied, "I am the servant of the Lord. May everything happen to me as you have said."

She had put her whole heart into her answer. She totally accepted God's plan.

The angel Gabriel had completed his mission. He left the young woman to return to the glory of God. From his place in heaven, he watched Mary visit her cousin Elizabeth; he heard the two women rejoicing together over the goodness of the Lord to mankind. Since Gabriel was an angel, and angels see what is hidden from men, he also saw the two babies, John and Jesus, greeting each other from their mothers' wombs.

Then came the time of joyous expectation. Even the angels, for whom a thousand years are like one day, couldn't wait to see the birth of the Savior of the world!

Joseph's Dreams

When Joseph, Mary's fiancé, learned that she was expecting a baby, he was very sad. Who was the father of this child? he wondered. Why had Mary betrayed him? He had been so happy to be engaged to her, and now his happiness was shattered. Joseph imagined that Mary must be in love with some other man, and that caused him great pain.

But Joseph was generous. He didn't want to hurt Mary out of jealousy. One evening, with his head in his hands, he prayed for a long time, asking God to show him what he should do for the good of all. In the end, he decided to break off the engagement very quietly.

"Tomorrow I'll go to see Mary and her parents," he thought to himself.

Joseph went to bed and, calmed by this wise decision, managed to fall asleep. An angel leaned over him as he dreamed. He looked at the sleeping man with a smile. Poor Joseph! He had dark rings under his eyes from all his worries, but his face was peaceful, like that of a just man. He resembled his ancestor King David, thought the angel, who had been watching men for centuries. He saw in this carpenter of Nazareth some features of the great king of Israel, but his hair was a little less ruddy than David's.

Without waking Joseph, the angel spoke to him: "Joseph, do not be afraid to take Mary as your wife, for the child she is expecting is from God. You will call him Jesus, which means 'God saves,' for he will save people from their sins."

Joseph didn't open his eyes, but a smile crept over his lips. The angel left without a sound. He knew that from then on the Lord could count on Joseph to protect Mary and the child.

And that is just what happened. Joseph married Mary and watched over her. When the time for her to give birth was nearing, Emperor Augustus ordered everyone to go to his hometown to be counted. The couple had to leave for Bethlehem, the city of David, for Joseph to enroll in the census. It was there, in a stable, that Mary gave birth to Jesus. There was great joy in heaven! God sent an angel to announce the good news to some shepherds who were keeping watch over their sheep in the nearby fields. Then a whole host of angels appeared to them in the sky. They sang, "Glory to God," and the night sky echoed with their wonderful song.

The angel who had appeared to Joseph watched him as he bent over the manger where baby Jesus was sleeping. Joseph loved this child with all his heart and all his might. The angel could see it in his face.

A little later, after the three wise men had come to pay homage to Jesus, the same angel returned to Joseph. It was nighttime and Joseph was asleep. The angel wasted no time, for his mission was urgent: Jesus was in great danger. He said to Joseph: "Rise up. Take the child and his mother and flee to Egypt. Stay there until I let you know when to return, for King Herod is seeking the child to put him to death."

Joseph woke with a start. He looked about for the angel, but saw no one except his wife and son. Quickly, he set them on the donkey that had carried them to Bethlehem. The only baggage he took were the coffers offered the day before by the wise men, filled with gold, frankincense, and myrrh; he couldn't bring himself to leave behind these gifts given to the Son of God. Then they disappeared into the night.

Jesus and his parents stayed in Egypt for some years. At last, one night in a dream, Joseph recognized the angel who had already come to him twice before. In a joyful voice, the messenger of God told him: "Rise up, take the child and his mother and return to the land of Israel, for those who sought to take the child's life have died."

Joseph woke up. He didn't even wait for dawn to wake Mary and Jesus. All three left right away and headed for Galilee. Joseph was so happy, he hummed in the night the psalm his ancestor David had written: "Awake, my harp, I will awaken the dawn."

Mary and Jesus smiled on hearing this song of joy, and the angel did, too.

The Angel at the Tomb

The sun was rising, and the rosy sky promised a lovely day. But for the two women walking with heavy steps to the cemetery, it was still night—a black and terrible night that had begun the day before yesterday, on Friday. That day, there was darkness over all the land from noon until three o'clock, when Jesus died. After that, for most of the people of Jerusalem, life went back to normal. But for Mary Magdalene and another Mary, both faithful friends of Jesus, it felt as though there would never again be any brightness on earth.

At least, that is what they thought as they made their way with heads bowed. Jesus was the Light of the world. Now that he had been put to death, the sun could never shine enough to brighten their lives.

Mary Magdalene and the other Mary entered the cemetery and headed to the back of the garden. In caves carved into the rock were the tombs of the wealthy of Jerusalem. A generous admirer of Jesus, Joseph of Arimathea, had bought a burial place for himself there. When Jesus was crucified, he asked the Roman governor Pontius Pilate for permission to place his body in this empty tomb.

"Jesus was born like a poor man in a stable, and he died like a criminal on a cross. Yet here he is buried among the wealthy," said Mary Magdalene in a low voice.

The other Mary nodded her head but suddenly exclaimed, "The stone! Who is going to roll the stone away from the entrance for us?"

The two women stopped for a moment, perplexed. They looked at the jars of spices they had brought with them to anoint Jesus' body. Would they even be able to get into the tomb? On Friday, it had taken the combined strength of several men to roll the enormous stone across the entrance to the tomb. They were just two women, tired out from two long, sleepless nights. They would never have the strength to do it by themselves!

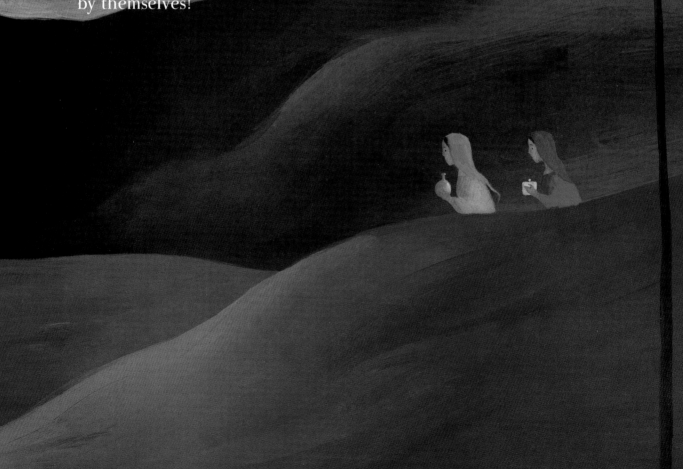

But when they arrived at the tomb, they saw that the enormous block had already been rolled away to one side. They were speechless with amazement. The entrance to the cave was open before them, completely black, like the color of their sorrow. They went into the tomb and, on the right, saw a stranger. His clothing was as white as snow. His presence lit up the tomb. The air around him did not smell of death.

Mary clutched her jar tightly. Mary Magdalene looked at the carefully folded linen cloths in a corner of the tomb. These were the cloths they had wrapped Jesus in, but Jesus wasn't there any more. Terrified, Mary stifled a cry.

Then the stranger said, "Do not be afraid!"

His gentle voice echoed in the empty tomb. His accent didn't sound like that of someone from Galilee, or from any other region of the country. So the two women guessed that he must come from another world, from the kingdom of heaven. He was an angel, a messenger of God.

The angel went on, saying, "You are looking for Jesus of Nazareth, the crucified one? He has risen; he is not here. Come and see the place where his body was laid." The angel pointed to the stone bench on which he was seated.

"And now," he added, "go tell Peter and the other disciples that Jesus has risen from the dead and will meet them in Galilee.

The women dropped their precious jars, and the scent of spices filled the tomb, where there was no longer anyone to anoint: Even the angel had suddenly disappeared. They backed out of the cave. Then they took to their heels at full speed, wild with astonishment and fear, not yet daring to believe the words that had been spoken to them.

But as they ran back through the garden, the first rays of sunlight lit up the green spring grass, and hope crept into the hearts of the two women. Jesus had risen, truly risen! Then Jesus himself appeared to them. The love of God had indeed been stronger than death. Jesus was alive! Even more than before, Jesus was the Light of the world.

Printed in June 2017 by Tien Wah Press (Malaysia)
Job number MGN17015
Printed in compliance with the Consumer Protection Safety Act, 2008.